THE FARM

PHOTOGRAPHS BY

REUBEN SALLOWS AND JOHN DE VISSER

TEXT BY JOCK CARROLL

Methuen

TORONTO   NEW YORK   LONDON   SYDNEY   AUCKLAND

Canadian Cataloguing in Publication Data

Sallows, Reuben, 1855–1937
   The farm

ISBN 0-458-97900-7

1. Agriculture – Ontario – History –
Pictorial works. 2. Farm life – Ontario –
History – Pictorial works. 3. Agriculture
– Ontario – History. I. De Visser, John,
1930– II. Carroll, Jock, 1919– III. Title.

S522.C2S24 1984   630'.9713   C84-099058-8

Design: The Dragon's Eye Press

Printed and bound in Canada
1 2 3 4   84   88 87 86 85

SPONSORS:

Ciba-Geigy Canada Ltd. and Funk Seeds

H.J. Heinz Company of Canada Ltd.

Ontario Federation of Agriculture

Ontario Ministry of Agriculture and Food

CO-SPONSORS:

Campbell Soup Company Ltd

John Labatt Limited

CONTENTS

INTRODUCTION

A photograph freezes a moment in time, capturing a mood, stopping an action, preserving forever one infinitesimal tick of history's clock. Glancing at these frozen moments, we see them come to life again as the photographs evoke sights and smells and sounds, releasing images in our mind's eye.

So it is with these views of agriculture past and present. These photographs bring to us once again the sounds and the sweat, the tears and the triumphs of the struggle to bring forth food from an often reluctant, sometimes hostile environment. They also underline the dramatic changes that have taken place as agriculture in Ontario moved from the horse to high-tech, from brute force to big business. At the same time, these pictures are a celebration of a special breed of people as they pursue a special way of life.

Many things change. Some things never do. Agriculture remains a fluid and delicate balance between the weather, the land and the spirit and determination of the people who work the land.

And it is to those on the land in Ontario, past and present, that this book is respectfully and gratefully dedicated.

DENNIS TIMBRELL
Minister of Agriculture and Food

THE PHOTOGRAPHERS

REUBEN SALLOWS (1855–1937) was one of Canada's great pioneer photographers. He began his work in 1879, when most photography was limited to stiff, studio portraits because of heavy cameras, tripods and slow exposure times.

Sallows later ventured from his studio to photograph people in their natural surroundings, including farmers at work in the fields. This work brought him quick recognition, and soon he was commissioned to travel to western Canada and as far north as the Arctic to photograph settlers, Indians, Doukhobors and Eskimos. His base remained at Goderich, however, and the photos in this book are from that area.

His work is an invaluable documentary record of the changing patterns of agriculture. Although most of his work was realistic, Sallows was not above staging the occasional photo to dramatize some aspect of rural life which appealed to him.

Sallows's photos were recorded on glass-plate negatives, measuring 5 × 7 or 6 × 8 inches. By 1916 Sallows had a stock of more than 6000 irreplaceable scenes, but unfortunately many of the glass plates were lost after his death. He was killed in a car accident at the age of 82, on his way to another assignment.

JOHN DE VISSER emigrated from The Netherlands in 1952 and became a Canadian citizen and a full-time freelance photographer as soon as time and circumstances permitted. He lives in a one-hundred-year-old house in Port Hope.

His photographs have appeared in most major Canadian magazines, as well as in *Time, Life, Newsweek, Der Stern, Paris-Match, National Geographic* and other publications.

He has contributed to the National Film Board books *Canada: A Year of the Land* and *Between Friends,* and has had fifteen books of his own photographs published. Of these his favorite is *This Rock Within the Sea,* done with Farley Mowat.

De Visser does not see himself as a director of photographs, in the style of studio or fashion photography, but rather as one who reacts to the colour and beauty in life. He is probably best known for his colour landscapes.

He works with several cameras but does much of his work with two 35 mm Nikons constantly to hand, loaded with Kodachrome 64 film.

His many awards include the NFB Gold Medal for Still Photography and an Eastman Kodak Special Award for colour photography. He is an elected member of the Royal Canadian Academy of Fine Arts.

PREVIOUS PAGES
(in order of appearance)

A warm summer day finds cattle grazing in the rolling hills near Campbellford.

*

Pioneer farmers had a good sugar substitute once they'd mastered the art of making maple sugar. After the pails of sap had been boiled down to maple syrup in evaporating pans inside the sugar house, the final step took place outside. Here the syrup was boiled further in iron kettles to the point of granulation, a tricky step that had to be tended carefully. Note the ingenious use of cleft branches to suspend the kettles over the fire.

*

On a hot, hazy day the Northumberland Hills fade into the distance.

*

Decorated pumpkins were as much a sign of Hallowe'en in 1915 as they are today.

THE LAND

PREVIOUS PAGES

(in order of appearance)

Farm life follows the rhythm of the
seasons and of the day. The first light of
dawn is reflected from the waters of
a stream.

*

As the land cools, hoar frost makes its
appearance.

The story of farming is the story of civilization. The human race has been traced back some 500000 years, but until very recently wandered the earth as hunters, clad in the skins of animals and living from day to day. Only when a few tribes decided to settle down in a favourable place, build shelters and cultivate crops was the basis for civilization laid down.

Similarly, the future of Ontario began to take shape with the wave of United Empire Loyalists who arrived following the American Revolution. To their grants of land some of the early loyalists brought livestock and farm equipment. But many had to be provided with primitive tools and food until they could begin to produce their own.

What kind of land did they find? It was a vast land of over 400000 square miles, or approximately 1000000 square kilometres. It was a land of rugged beauty. It was also a land of abundant water. Over 200000 inland lakes were linked by a network of streams and rivers which could provide clean drinking water, power for grist and sawmills and a transportation system far in advance of the roads and railways to come.

There were already farmers on the land. For a long time the Indians had grown maize, beans, squash and tobacco and had practised a kind of nomadic farming along with their hunting and fishing. There were also French farms in the Windsor area producing various crops and pioneering in the cultivation of peach, plum, apple and pear trees.

The new territory the loyalists were to settle was a very fertile land. Lord Durham later wrote that "it was considered the best grain country in North America." Unfortunately, it was largely covered with trees: in the south, black walnut, maple, elm, beech, ash and oak; in the north, spruce, balsam, cedar and red and white pine. Depending on his grant, his farm animals and his energy, an early settler might be lucky to clear five acres a year. It took nearly three generations to clear much of southern Ontario.

Roads to join the isolated settlements were an immediate problem. On Governor Simcoe's arrival at York he initiated the building of Yonge Street north from the lake and of the Dundas Road from York to London. He foresaw an eastward continuation of this to Lower Canada, and in 1799 Asa Danforth, an immigrant from the United States, contracted to cut the Danforth Trail, thirty-three feet wide, from York to the Bay of Quinte, a distance of 120 miles. He was to be paid $90 a mile, a reasonable price compared to the five million dollars a mile it costs for some of today's multilane highways.

In addition, it was agreed that Danforth's axemen would be given

200-acre land grants along the road when it was completed, a task that took ten years.

But government officials refused to make the land grants, and Danforth himself had difficulty in collecting his money. Somewhat embittered, he returned to the U.S., where he wrote a pamphlet complaining of the treatment he'd received in Upper Canada.

It seems fitting that a twentieth-century Ontarian, the late Marshall McLuhan, should develop the concept of the world as a global village, because from the beginning the province was strongly affected by foreign events, particularly in Europe. Napoleon's blockade cut Britain off from Scandinavian lumber badly needed for its navy, and British ships now streamed to Canada for lumber. The forests along the banks of the Ottawa and its tributaries began to ring with the sound of axes. A booming lumber trade provided jobs and created sawmills, as well as fortunes for a few. By the middle of the century the province was earning one million dollars a year – about 28 percent of all revenue – from lumber.

The ships coming for lumber brought successive waves of immigrants, refugees of the Scottish clearances and the Irish potato famines. In 1812 the population of Ontario was only 75 000, but it now doubled every twelve years and by 1860 reached 1.4 million. The growth in industry and population created needs for new and improved transportation. More roads appeared. The golden age of canal building was followed by the age of the railroads.

All these changes affected the farmer. New lands were opened to cultivation, and new markets for farm products began to appear both here and abroad. The province developed in the direction the early loyalists had set, for it was their strong desire to own and farm their own land that had changed the province from a crossroads for the canoes of the fur traders to a growing community of farm-supported settlements.

TOP LEFT:

Sunlight picks up the colours of autumn.

*

BOTTOM LEFT:

A plume of dust follows a car along a road
through cornfields near Cavan.

*

RIGHT:

Bales of hay dot this field near Earlton.

LEFT:

Judging by the white feathering
and white blazes on the foreheads,
the horses at the stream
for a cooling drink are Clydesdales,
a long-time Ontario favorite.

*

RIGHT:

Buckets of sap are collected
in a drum for hauling to the sugar house.
When cheap imported sugar
appeared in the nineteenth century,
production of maple sugar fell off, with
most of the sap being used
for syrup.

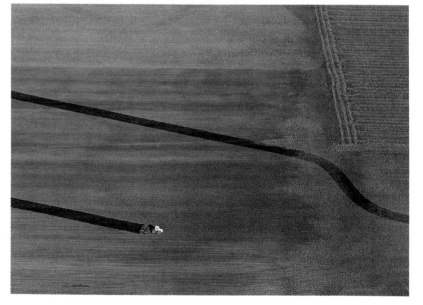

ABOVE:

Winter has brought stillness to this field, but elsewhere the work of the farm goes on.

✳

LEFT:

Perhaps the farmer making this puzzling pattern was testing his equipment or ploughing a contour.

THE PEOPLE

This 1908 farmer uses a hand drill to plant corn, one seed at a time.

The first farmers of Upper Canada were the Indians, who had been growing crops for many years before the arrival of the Europeans. Also predating the loyalists was a good-sized French farming community along the banks of the Detroit River between Sandwich and Amherstberg. The Pajot farm near La Salle is believed to be the oldest farm in Ontario, having been worked by that family since 1772.

The ten thousand loyalists who came to the land west of the Ottawa River after the Revolution pointed to the multicultural future of what became Ontario. They included descendants of English Puritans, the Roman Catholic Glengarry Highlanders, German-speaking Mennonites, disbanded Hessian soldiers, the Pennsylvania Dutch, a sprinkling of French Huguenots and others.

Peter Secord, who fought with Butler's Rangers, is believed to be the first loyalist farmer, taking a land grant near Niagara in the early 1780s. His niece, Laura Secord, became a legend of the War of 1812.

The largest group of loyalists, however, is often overlooked – the Indians of the Six Nations, who fought for the British, lost their land south of the Great Lakes and were granted a block of some 67 500 acres along the Grand River near Brantford and acreage near Deseronto.

Generous grants were made to ex-soldiers, depending on rank: a private received 100 acres, with 50 more for his wife and 50 for each child; officers' grants were larger, up to 5000 acres for field officers.

Some loyalists managed to bring livestock, furniture and farm tools with them. The government did its best to provide the others with basic tools: a broadaxe, mattock, shovel, hoe, scythe, saw and musket. Clothes, seed wheat and rations of salt pork were provided for the first year and often longer.

There were few towns, mostly military bases, but the contrast between life there and on the farm was striking. The diary of Mrs. Simcoe, the Lieutenant Governor's wife, has left us sketches of Toronto in the three years Simcoe spent there, when he re-named it York and prepared to make it the capital of the new colony. The garrison of two hundred Queen's Rangers formed the bulk of the town's population at first, but they were gradually joined by officials, merchants and tradespeople. By 1800 the gentry enjoyed a kind of social life patterned on England's, including foxhunts and duels. In January of that year Upper Canada's first Attorney-General, John White, was killed in a shootout with John Small, Clerk of the Executive Council.

But for farmers, particularly inexperienced ones, the first years were grim. The winter of 1788–89 became known as "The Hungry Year," with some settlers literally starving to death. There was much that had to be done to ensure survival. The clearing of a "wheat piece" was essential, but even before that many families had to cut trees for a one-room log cabin, using only primitive tools against the deadline of approaching winter. The chinks in the logs had to be filled with mud and straw.

Firewood had to be cut and chopped for warmth and for cooking, which was done with a few pots and kettles suspended in a crude fireplace. For light, the pioneers learned to make candles from animal fat. For soap, they learned to leach lye from wood ashes. For sugar, they learned to tap the maple.

There were blessings. Deer and other animals ran the woods, the waters teemed with fish, and wildfowl flew overhead. But hunting took time, and there were periods when families existed on little but milk, bread and potatoes.

The farm wife coped heroically with these conditions, often while looking after several small children, with another one on the way. There was the ever-present danger of accident, sickness or death in the family.

Some women were used to rough conditions; others suffered from culture shock. One such was Susanna Moodie, wife of a British officer, who came to Canada in 1832. She described her adventures in a classic book, *Roughing It in the Bush,* telling how she learned to make pie from the flesh of black squirrels and coffee from roasted dandelion roots.

But these men and women were resourceful and independent, driven by a hunger to possess their own land and to prosper by the work of their own hands.

There was a unity to family life and a sense of common purpose difficult to maintain today. The whole family shared in the work of the farm, in its joys and sorrows, triumphs and disasters.

LEFT:

Sallows brought together all the elements of a classic farm scene – two dapple greys pulling a hand plow, the thirsty farmer and the welcome dipper of cold water brought by a loving son. An experienced farmer might note the field already appears to have been harrowed.

*

RIGHT:

Sallows took this picture of hand planting in 1907. It's likely the family is planting cabbage seedlings. The small tufts of white are paper collars fastened around the seedlings to protect them from the larva of the cabbage fly.

PREVIOUS PAGE:

Modern machinery has revolutionized farm work, but has not entirely
replaced the use of hand tools.

One man turns the grindstone, while the other sharpens the scythe blade.
Many a backwoods pioneer tackled the problem of land clearance with a
handful of tools: an axe, broadaxe, pick, shovel, scythe and perhaps a
grindstone shared with a few adjacent neighbours.

ABOVE:

Harvesting wheat with a binder was hot work in 1908.

*

LEFT:

Cutting grain with a scythe called for a keen edge. The wooden cradle
attachment to the scythe scoops the cut grain into piles.

19

TOP LEFT:
Oxen were still in use in 1907 in some parts of the province. This hay was probably baled with one of the early, steam-powered, mechanical hay balers, which were stationary in the field.

*

BOTTOM LEFT:
These apple barrels must be empties on their way to the orchard, otherwise the horses would not be having such an easy time of it.

*

RIGHT:
Young people have long been drawn to the cities, but many still enjoy the challenge and outdoor work of the farm.

"Back-breaking" would seem to be the proper term for pulling flax by
hand. The best fibres for linen were in the stalk close to the root.

ABOVE:

When wheat was sown by hand.

✳

TOP RIGHT:

Growing flax to make grain-bags,
household linen and coarse clothing was
a laborious process. First, it had to be
hand-pulled, as this group of
Indian workers appears to be doing.
Then followed weathering of the stalks,
crushing, separation of the woody
remnants from the fibre and hackling with
combs of increasing fineness. Today's crop
is grown for flaxseed.

✳

BOTTOM RIGHT:

Judging by the finished rows to left and
right, these workers are pulling onion
sets to be used as seed onions next season.

ABOVE:

A happy girl returns from the prize ring with a red ribbon on her pony.

∗

RIGHT:

This girl in her high-button shoes does not appear nervous, but perhaps

this ewe is a pet of hers.

24

TOP LEFT:

Tame animals were one of the joys of life on the farm. This pet crow seems to have become one of the family.

*

BOTTOM LEFT:

Farm youngsters all dressed up for a ride in a training cart.

*

RIGHT:

A classic Thanksgiving scene which seems to have been stage-managed by Sallows, with directions to the little girl. Grandpa is definitely *not* demonstrating the safest way to behead a turkey.

TOP LEFT:

You can bring your calf to the fall fair, but you can't always persuade it to march around the ring on its best behaviour, as this young exhibitor discovered at the Wiarton Fair in the Bruce Peninsula.

✳

BOTTOM LEFT:

A farmer in the Great Clay Belt stands proudly in front of his cattle.

✳

RIGHT:

A farmer trims a prized calf for a show ring appearance.

Two very well-dressed dairymaids put milk through the separator to produce cream for buttermaking. Sallows probably moved this operation to the orchard to include the spring blossoms.

*

A home-made apple pie in the making. In Ontario's early days, the apple was the fruit of all seasons, eaten from summer harvest time till late next spring.

*

Selected apples were firmly pressed into wooden apple barrels for shipment with this apple press. The old thirty-cent apple barrel has now given way to cardboard cartons.

LEFT:

This log cabin near Maberley is typical
of the earliest Ontario farm homes.

*

BELOW:

A typical early farm house near Vankleek.
The life of a farm woman was hard and,
before modern communications, often a
lonely one.

ABOVE:
Grandpa has his whiskers trimmed,
perhaps for an appearance at church.

*

LEFT:
Emergency repairs.

*

RIGHT:
This milkmaid has her hand on a dual-
purpose Durham cow, for years a
common dairy breed in Ontario.

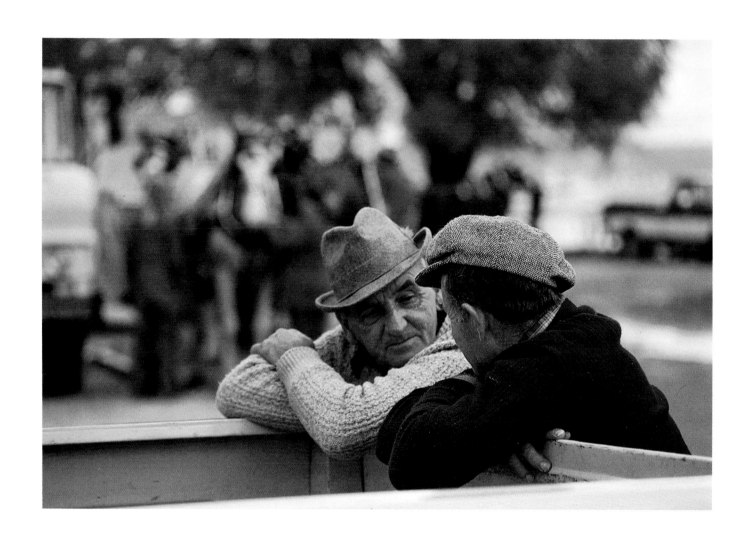

ABOVE:

Fairs and exhibitions bring farmers together to compete and to learn
how neighbours are doing.

*

RIGHT:

Thawing out the pump was a winter chore.

LEFT:

Before the appearance of cultivated fruit, some early settlers were able
to supplement their diets with wild strawberries, raspberries and
blackberries.

*

ABOVE:

A quick-stepping horse and fancy buggy preceded the appearance
of the flivver.

LEFT:

Sallows has used a makeshift butter churn and a touch of romance to indicate that life was not all work and no play.

*

BELOW:

Even scarecrows come to the fair. Luckily, this one being carried to the fair at Port Hope can't talk.

THE CROPS

A forage harvester works a hayfield near Rainy River.

For many years the settlers serving the French garrison at Detroit had grown wheat, barley, oats, peas, Indian corn and potatoes. They also had small orchards of pear, peach, apple, plum and cherry trees. But the new wave of English-speaking settlers cleared the land with one main crop in mind: wheat. Not only was it needed for bread, but it could also be used for barter.

In clearing and burning the trees from their future wheatfields, many farmers discovered their first cash crop – potash that could be leached from the ashes of burned hardwoods. Potash was in demand in Europe for the manufacture of soaps, fertilizers and gunpowder, and by December of 1799 a merchant could advertise in the *Upper Canada Gazette:*

Ashes!   Ashes!   Ashes!

and announce that his potashery was paying seven pence per bushel for fireplace ashes and eight pence for field ashes. Large quantities of the latter were produced at "burning bees," when farmers rid themselves of trees cut from their land. It took an acre of good hardwood to produce a barrel of pure potash worth perhaps $100.

For the family's own use the backwoods farmer planted potatoes, turnips and corn. Later, there would be rye for the local distillery. But the most important crop remained wheat. For more than half a century the grain was the engine of economic growth. As far back as 1794 Lieutenant Governor Simcoe had suggested a currency based on flour.

There were many good reasons for the dominance of wheat. The land and climate were eminently suitable, and even before the fields were properly cleared a crop could be had by clearing the brush and girdling the trees or burning them at their base. The virgin land yielded crops as high as forty bushels an acre.

Wheat meant survival for the farm family, as it could be sown, harvested, threshed and winnowed by hand. And before the first grist mills appeared, it could be pounded into a kind of brown flour with home-made mortars and pestles. Kept dry, wheat did not deteriorate in storage or transit and could be carried in a bag slung over the farmer's shoulder. There were problems, however. Early varieties were plagued by black stem rust and a gnat-like fly called the midge. A transplanted Scot named David Fife produced one rust-resistant strain he called Red Fife, which was later combined with Hard Red Calcutta to produce the famous Marquis wheat.

The opening of export markets in the United Kingdom and the United

States reinforced wheat as the main cash crop, and until the early 1860s it produced three-quarters of the farm's income. At the same time, wheat or flour was the source of one-half of Ontario's export income.

But the wheat economy was in trouble. There had been little crop rotation or fertilization, and soil exhaustion cut crop yields in half. The day of the "wheat miner," who simply opened up new land to compensate for diminishing yields, was coming to an end. There was also increasing competition in wheat markets from the United States and the Canadian west. By the early 1880s the Ontario acreage devoted to wheat was steadily declining.

Fortunately there was a growing awareness of the importance of more scientific farming methods. Here and there individual farmers imported purebred strains of pigs, sheep and beef and dairy cattle. Fall fairs, county fairs and provincial exhibitions brought farmers together for an exchange of ideas. And many agricultural societies were formed, the Agricultural Association of Upper Canada being established as early as 1846.

There was a giant step forward in 1868 when John Carling was appointed Commissioner of Agriculture and Public Works. This led to the founding of the first Agricultural College at Guelph, which was eventually followed by five more as well as the Ontario Veterinary College. Today the province is dotted with experimental stations, and every county in Ontario has its trained agricultural representative.

Following quickly this expansion of agricultural knowledge was the revolution that came with the introduction of modern farm machinery. Pioneer farmers worked hard to provide food for themselves and their families. Today, the average Ontario farmer provides food for nearly a hundred people.

Wheat once dominated Ontario farming.

*

RIGHT:

A combine at work near New Liskeard creates an abstract pattern in
a swathed field of grain.

The two years separating these photos show how
mechanization of the farm progressed. On the left the hay-loader is
operated by horse power; on the right it is the horsepower
of a kerosene-fuelled tractor.

LEFT:

A forage harvester at work in a cornfield
near Mountain View.

*

BELOW:

Grain pours from a combine
near Englehart.

TOP LEFT:

A cultivator, pulled by a three-horse team, breaks up the land for seeding.

*

BOTTOM LEFT:

This kerosene-fuelled Titan 10-20 tractor, here pulling a three-furrow plough, came into use around the end of World War I. The 10 refers to the horsepower on the pull; the 20 to the horsepower on the power take-off belt.

*

RIGHT:

This ploughman is operating a very early kerosene-fuelled tractor in 1916. Rubber tires did not appear on tractors till much later.

LEFT:

A regional ploughing match brings out an
early gasoline-powered tractor.

*

TOP RIGHT:

A modern tobacco-harvesting machine.

*

BOTTOM RIGHT:

Flue-cured tobacco is a multi-million
dollar crop for farmers in the
Simcoe – Delhi area.

LEFT:

Burley tobacco such as this was the common crop before World War I. It was used for cigars and pipe-smoking, but largely as chewing tobacco. Flue-cured tobacco for cigarettes now dominates and is approximately a $250 000 000 per year crop in Ontario.

*

TOP RIGHT:

Here's how that crop of Swedish turnips got planted in the spring: two rows sown at a time with a single-horse seed drill. Seeds were tripped from the cannisters ahead of the rollers.

*

BOTTOM RIGHT:

A wagonload of rutabaga or Swedish turnips, usually the last crop brought in, because it was thought they were improved by a touch of frost. These have been topped first, then dug out by hand, harrow or plough.

*

FOLLOWING PAGE:

A field of sunflowers in the Mennonite area near Kitchener.

ABOVE:

In early times pumpkins were stored in the barn for winter cattle feed.
Later, pumpkin pie came into favour.

*

RIGHT:

Grandpa separates potato sprouts which have become overlong and
tangled. The potato is one of the vegetables indigenous to this
hemisphere. Originally found in Peru, it was taken to Europe, then
migrated back to North America with the early settlers.

ABOVE:

The approach of Hallowe'en has brought
out this crop of pumpkins near Markham.

✳

RIGHT:

Decorative gourds for sale at a roadside
stand at Brighton.

LEFT:

These 1910 farmers look for a prize-winner for the fall fair.

ABOVE:

These championship squashes were grown by William Warnock of
Goderich in 1904. The exhibitor, wearing a ribbon,
seems to have put on his Sunday best in anticipation of a prize.

Sunshine is vital to the grape, and new varieties are
improving the Ontario wine industry.

*

TOP RIGHT:

Blossom time in the fruit belt.

*

BOTTOM RIGHT:

Peaches ready for market.

In 1905 derby hats could still be seen in the orchard. These sorters grade
apples for colour, size, disease and damage before packing, as one rotten
apple can spoil a barrel.

This 1910 farmer is about to load a sleigh with bark for delivery to the
local tannery. After use in the tanning process the spent bark might see
further use as the "tanbark" in a circus ring.

ABOVE:

Maple sap drips from an old-fashioned spigot at Kemptville.

*

LEFT:

Tapping the maple was learned from the Indians. The final
stage of boiling syrup to the granulation point had to be carefully
watched and was usually done by women. In this 1910 photo the final
product is being ladled into the sugar moulds.

Winter was the time to sleigh logs from the woodlot to the sawmill,
as snow made large loads practical for a two-horse team.
The white pine, staple of the timber trade, has now been declared
the official tree of Ontario.

The big pine is down. To keep the crosscut saw from binding, the man
in the centre is tapping wedges in with a maul. The timber industry, based
largely on the white pine, provided shelter, furniture, industries and jobs
and led to the creation of transportation networks. Throughout the
1800s it was the largest single source of revenue.

TOP:

Market gardeners at work in the famous rich black soil of Holland Marsh.

*

BOTTOM:

Growers and buyers come together at London's Farmer's Market.

THE ANIMALS

The first white explorers who stumbled across America in their search for the riches of the Orient found no domestic animals with the Indians who greeted them, other than dogs meant for eating on ceremonial occasions.

It was the colonists who followed the explorers who brought cattle, horses, sheep and poultry from Europe – the Spanish to their bases in the Caribbean and Central America, the British to their colonies along the Atlantic seaboard and the French to their settlements around the mouth of the St. Lawrence. From these early stocks came the farm animals which, with the settlers, gradually pushed inland.

Those few animals which had reached Upper Canada 200 years ago were very valuable, despite a lack of pedigree. In 1793, for example, there arrived in York a New Englander named Charles Annis. With him he brought his wife, his children, a yoke of oxen, a mare, a colt and a heifer. In exchange for the heifer Annis was offered a hundred-acre lot on Yonge Street, including the land on which the Eaton Centre now stands. Annis turned down this offer and settled instead on a lot in the wilds of Scarborough – a decision his descendants may have since pondered.

Ten years earlier, on the seventeen farms scattered along the Niagara frontier, there were only 61 head of cattle, 30 sheep and 103 hogs. Today, Ontario has some 82 000 farms with 2 726 000 cattle, 245 000 sheep and lambs and 3 450 000 pigs.

This remarkable growth in livestock came about slowly. Backwoods farmers were happy with a few animals for their own needs, being intent on clearing the land for wheat. Indeed, there were so few animals in Upper Canada that one of the ironies of the War of 1812 was that many British garrisons were dependent on Yankee suppliers. By 1814 two-thirds of the men under arms in Canada were being fed with flour, beef and pork shipped from New York, Vermont and New Hampshire by enterprising Americans. This annoyed U.S. military commanders, but they did not have enough troops to police the borders.

Until 1850 Ontario farmers were more interested in improving their horses than in other livestock. In 1836 a few purebred draught horses were imported – Shires and Clydesdales – with the latter becoming a favorite in the next few decades.

Interest in the raising of cattle, sheep and pigs, however, was stimulated by a Reciprocity Treaty with the United States in 1854, which lasted until near the end of the American Civil War. Mutton, wool and beef found a ready market south of the border.

By Confederation, there were many breeds of cattle in the province – Ayrshires, Durhams, Devons, Herefords, Jerseys from the Royal Herd at

Windsor, Guernseys from the Channel Islands and Holstein-Friesians from Holland.

A burgeoning market in butter and cheese focused attention on dairy cattle. In the early days there had been local makers of cheese, but one man who helped turn cheese production into an industry was Hiram Ranney, an expatriate American who settled near Ingersol in 1841. From the milk of five cows tended by his wife, he made cheese and peddled it himself to surrounding towns. Some twelve years later he had 102 cows and a flourishing business.

Dairy farming also had the further advantage of providing year-round work for farmers, reducing their dependence on wheat. And in the next decade, with expanding domestic and export markets, cheese factories began springing up at an incredible rate. Some factories picked up the milk from local farmers, other farmers formed co-op factories and brought in the milk themselves. Buttermaking did not lag far behind; some preferred it, as the buttermilk could be fed to pigs.

Cheesemaking continued to surge ahead. By 1867 there were 235 factories making cheese in Ontario; by 1883 there were 635. In 1893, for the World's Exposition in Chicago, cheesemakers at Perth produced the biggest cheese on earth – six feet high, twenty-eight feet around and weighing thirteen tons. When it was unloaded in Chicago the mammoth cheese crashed through its supporting platform but survived this accident to win all prizes. After the Exposition it was bought by Sir Thomas Lipton and shipped to England.

Bessie, the farmer's cow, has come a long way in 200 years. Ontario is now famous for the milk production of its cows, and each year some 10 000 dairy breeding cattle are shipped to other parts of the world.

Beef cows and calves are on pasture near Goderich.
The lack of horns indicate they are Aberdeen Angus, the first purebred
herd of which was established at the experimental farm
in Guelph in 1876. "Eyebright 2nd,"
born there in 1877, was the first of the breed born in the
New World.

Early morning sunshine and fog near New Liskeard.

*

Outlined by sunshine, cattle stand out against a background of cedars.

There was no end to the chores of the farm wife. This one provides a
welcome drink for Durham calves.

Oxen, easily fed, tractable and strong,
were long indispensable on the backwoods farm.
Not till after 1850 were they supplanted by the horse. This one,
with its hand-carved wooden yoke,
was photographed in 1907.

BELOW:

Barn and sky loom above a Holstein herd.

*

RIGHT:

Sunshine on a stretch of fence creates
unusual effects.

ABOVE:

Herds of beef and dairy cattle were common by 1900, but the pioneer
farmer had few animals, perhaps only a pair of oxen, a cow or two,
a few pigs and some chickens and geese.

*

RIGHT:

A pair of oxen and a logging chain is all this farmer needs to haul his
logs from the bush. Along the St. Lawrence, as in France, oxen were
yoked by the horns, but in Ontario hand-carved yokes generally rested
behind the horns ahead of the shoulders.

One of Ontario's vanishing elms towers
over a herd at Emo.

*

Even the shade of a rail fence is welcome
on a hot summer day.

*

Ontario had few flocks of sheep until 1850,
as there was little demand for mutton, and
wool prices were low.

It's springtime, and time for a bath so that the wool will be
clean for the shearing.

A popular sheep in Ontario was the fine-wooled Southdown, imported
from England. At one time there was a strong demand for our
Southdowns, Shropshires and Oxfords in the United States.

ABOVE:

A Mennonite horse and carriage on a road near St. Jacob's.

*

TOP RIGHT:

A horse trots across a snow-covered field at Consecon
in the Bay of Quinte area.

*

BOTTOM RIGHT:

Horses and buggies wait patiently outside a Mennonite
meeting house near Waterloo.

Another crop of wheat is in the making as the farmer drives his seed
drill across a well-cultivated field.

Before the appearance of the machine-driven manure spreader, it took

three horses to do the job.

ABOVE:

Vivid decoration of barns, as in this stylized stencil on a barn door, was
common in eastern Ontario.

∗

LEFT:

A matched pair make their appearance at the Wiarton Fair.

ABOVE:

When work had to be done in a hurry, it was all hands to the plough.

An acre was a good day's work for one person.

*

RIGHT:

Good, straight rows are the sign of a good farmer. This one uses his

home-made marker to set out rows for the corn planter.

ABOVE:

This piglet seems to be the runt of the litter and is therefore getting a
little special attention, with nourishment fed through a cow's horn.

✳

RIGHT:

On the farm the first fall of snow meant pig-killing time. The carcass
has been hauled up for dressing and the man on the right amuses himself
by blowing up the bladder.

A hen turkey and family are fed by a farm wife in apron and poke bonnet.

*

ABOVE:
It's spring, the orchard is in bloom, and this farm wife looks happy with
her new hatching of chickens.

This gaggle of goslings will produce goose feathers for pillows and
comforters and goose grease to use as a hand lotion.

THE BUILDINGS

"Century Farm" signs indicate a farm that has been owned and worked by the same family for at least one hundred years. There are over 6000 of them in Ontario. In this Bicentennial Year the Ministry of Food and Agriculture has been trying to identify 200-year-old farms also, and current indications are that there are less than a dozen.

Other nostalgic landmarks of farm life — the split-rail snake fence, the stump fence, the weathered barns, the creaking windmills, the lilac-framed homes of patterned brick or gingerbread gables — are also disappearing from the country roads. Fortunately they have long been favorite subjects of artists and photographers. Architects, too, have admired the functional simplicity, integrity and craftsmanship of farm buildings.

The first urgent need of the backwoods farmer was for shelter, and the first trees felled were often used to build a one-room log shanty without the benefit of nails. The shanty roof might be made of elm bark or, if there was time, of hollowed-out basswood poles overlapped in tile fashion. A crude fireplace could be made by heaping stones together, and a serviceable chimney could be fashioned of wattle-and-daub, or simply be a hole cut in the roof. In this one-room shanty the family cooked, ate and slept, while a "wheat piece" was cleared.

Planks for a floor might come later with the use of a pit-saw. A pit was dug, a log placed over it and the log sawn lengthwise with one man above the log and another down in the pit. Small wonder that sawmills were a priority for new farm communities.

It might be some years before a farmer could build an improved log cabin, with the logs hewn square by broad-axe or adze, or perhaps a board and batten house.

For some time the basic shape of the cabin was retained, repeated in stone or patterned brick, with perhaps the addition of a peaked gable for what came to be known as "The Ontario-Style House." More elaborate styles followed, with decorative bargeboarding or gingerbread dripping from the gables and festooning the verandahs.

The front parlour, even though little used, became a status symbol, sometimes furnished with carpets, lamps, reproductions of fine furniture, a horsehair sofa and a family album.

Ontario farmers prospered in the 1850s and 1860s, helped by an increasing domestic market and foreign markets opened up by the American Civil War and the Crimean War. By 1880 nearly half of the province's farmers lived in substantial frame, stone or brick homes.

More than half had first-class barns. The word "barn" was originally created from the Old English words *bere,* meaning barley, and *ern,* meaning place, and came to mean a place for the laying up of any sort of grain, hay or straw. After a cabin, the first need of the farmer was for a barn. It was essential for wheat, as the barn floor provided a place for separating the grain with hand flails and winnowing the wheat from the chaff with the aid of a breeze blowing through open barn doors.

The first barn was often of the same simple log construction as the cabin. Then it grew to include a granary, a lower level for horses and cattle and an upper level for hay and sheaves. The Ontario banked barn was common, built into the side of a hill or with a ramp to provide upper access.

Depending on the ancestry of the builder, barns showed different influences – the English Barn, the Dutch Barn or the Pennsylvania Barn. There were even a few round and polygonal barns.

The erection of a large barn was a task beyond a single farmer. This led to the traditional barn-raising bee where a score or even a hundred neighbours gathered to push and haul the barn framework into place. The farmer provided food and whiskey for the evening dance and festivities, often the only social life for isolated families.

The actual raising of the barn was preceded by much hard work: the preparation of a foundation, the felling of trees to be hewn square for posts and beams, and the careful mortise-and-tenon carpentry so that the timbers could be fastened together with wooden dowels. Before the actual raising, the skeleton of the barn, apart from the roof, would be readied on the ground.

Other farm buildings were created according to the needs and inclination of the individual farmer – a sugar house for maple syrup, a dairy barn, a carriage shed, a smoke house, a silo.

Many such old farm buildings remain, reflecting a way of life that is no longer with us. They are romantic reminders of an enduring agricultural tradition that has been the foundation of Ontario's development and the key to its prosperity.

A hay fork lifts the hay, and it is run back into the mow as the farmer
holds a trip rope. This rig saved pitching the hay several times to get it
to the back of the mow.

LEFT:

The light at the end of the road has cheered many a weary farmer over the years, a feeling evoked by the view of this farmhouse near the village of Baltimore.

✳

TOP RIGHT:

Even this home near Niagara-on-the-Lake, which contains some of the finest examples of early architecture in the province, resembles the basic log cabin of the first settlers.

✳

BOTTOM RIGHT:

Snow falls quietly on a farmhouse near Colborne with decorative "gingerbread" typical of another era.

Steam provided the power for early
portable sawmills. This huge tree has
already been cut into twelve-foot lengths
for boards.

A mighty barn rises from a fieldstone foundation. As many as one
hundred farmers gathered at barn-raising bees, which, along with apple-
paring bees, corn-husking bees and others, were sometimes the only
social occasions enjoyed by isolated farmers.

This 1912 beekeeper demonstrates the production of comb honey. Honey
bees were common in early settlements. The pioneering David A. Jones
of Beeton imported European strains of honey bees and isolated them on
islands in Georgian Bay beginning in 1870.

The windmill is another vanishing landmark. Used mainly for pumping
water, it occasionally powered small farm machinery.

Horses haul a sleigh carrying a drum of maple sap to the sugar house to
be boiled down to syrup. How much sap the pioneers required to make a
pound of maple sugar is unknown. Some estimate eight pounds, others
as much as forty pounds.

An early portable gasoline engine powers a corn chopper and silo filler.

Silos did not appear in Ontario until late in the nineteenth century.

Winter settles over the land, emphasizing the loneliness of a small
farmhouse.